48-HOUR
APPLIQUÉ QUILTS

by Linda Causee

Have you been afraid to try making an appliqué quilt because of all the sewing required to create one?

If so, we have news for you! Try fusing.

Using the fusible materials on the market today, you can become an appliqué quilt artist in no time. Just grab your iron and get started.

In this book, we've given you patterns for 74 beautiful quilt blocks which we have put together into five quilts. Since the patterns are the same size, you can mix and match the blocks into many quilts, or you can recreate the quilts that we show here.

If you're a beginner at using the fusing method, start with the Easy Appliqué Quilt on page 10. After you have become more proficient, you might want to try your hand at making the Faux Baltimore Album quilt on page 20. It's a great way to show off your newly learned skills and create a family heirloom at the same time.

Happy Fusing!

Produced for Leisure Arts by The Creative Partners™ LLC

CONTENTS

Carol Wilson Mansfield, Photo Stylist

Wayne Norton, Photography

Ann Harnden, Copy Editor

Graphic Solutions inc-chgo, Book Design

Produced by The Creative Partners™

Thanks to Wanda MacLachlan and Meredith Montross for helping to make the photographed quilts and Faith Horsky for her fine machine quilting.

Special thanks to the Warm™ Company for providing Steam-A-Seam 2® and Fairfield Processing Corp. for supplying Cotton Classic® batting for the projects.

GENERAL DIRECTIONS

PATTERNS

The patterns for the appliqué blocks can be found on pages 23 to 96. Tracing the patterns directly from the book will result in blocks that are 9" finished.

FABRICS

For several hundred years, quilts were made with 100% cotton fabric, and this remains the fabric choice for most quilters today. It is especially useful for hand appliqué. But for fusible appliqué, you can use other fabrics for the appliqués; refer to the manufacturer's directions for the fusible product that you are using for special instructions using non-cotton fabrics. It is best to use 100% cotton for the background blocks.

Many quilters do not prewash, but for fusible appliqué it is advised that you prewash all fabrics. It will allow the fabrics to bond together more thoroughly and completely. Do not use softening as it can interfere with the bonding process.

PAPER-BACKED FUSIBLE PRODUCTS

There are many different paper-backed fusible products on the market today. Each has its own unique characteristics that will help you decide which product to use when making your quilt.

Important: *Whichever product you use, be sure to carefully follow the manufacturer's directions as each differs greatly.*

Steam-A-Seam® by The Warm™ Company
This product has a pressure-sensitive coating on one side allowing a temporary hold to the appliqué fabric. You can leave the edges of your appliqués unfinished or you can machine stitch around the edges without gumming up the needle. Your quilt will be washable or dry cleanable after fusing. Use for heavier weight fabrics such as denim.

Lite Steam-A-Seam® by The Warm™ Company
This product has the same properties as Steam-A-Seam, but use it for sheer and lightweight fabrics such as 100% cotton.

Lite Steam-A-Seam 2® by The Warm™ Company
This product has a pressure-sensitive coating on both sides which allows a temporary hold until it is fused down permanently with an iron. It is great for multiple layers of appliqué as it forms a strong, permanent bond and leaves the fabric soft and pliable. You can leave the edges unfinished, but can machine stitch without gumming up your needle. Your quilt will be washable or dry cleanable after fusing.

Steam-A-Seam 2® by The Warm™ Company
This product has the same properties as Lite Steam-A-Seam® except it is intended for heavier fabrics.

Pellon® WonderUnder® Transfer Web
This product is designed for lightweight fabrics such as 100% cotton. Machine stitching around appliqué is recommended to make your quilt machine washable.

Pellon® Heavy-Duty WonderUnder® Transfer Web
This product is for heavier fabrics such as denim and canvas.

Therm O Web HeatnBond Lite® Iron-On Adhesive
This product is for lightweight fabrics such as 100% cotton. It will not add extra weight or stiffness to the fabric. Machine stitch around appliqués if you will be washing your quilt; your needle will not gum up.

Therm O Web HeatnBond® UltraHold Iron-On Adhesive
Use this product for heavier weight fabrics or for projects that will not require sewing.

PREPARING THE APPLIQUÉ PIECES

Trace patterns onto the fusible product following manufacturer's directions. Remember that pattern pieces that are not symmetrical will end up as mirror images in the finished project. (**Diagram 1**)

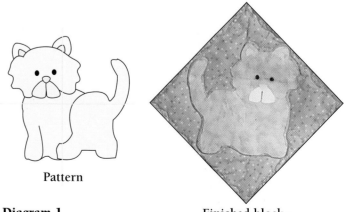

Pattern

Diagram 1

Finished block - a mirror image

Hint: First trace separate pattern pieces onto template plastic using a black permanent marker. If a piece is on top of another piece, extend shape of "under" piece so "over" piece will lie on top. (**Diagram 2**) Mark how many of each pattern piece you will need for the block. (**Diagram 3**) Cut out templates along drawn lines.

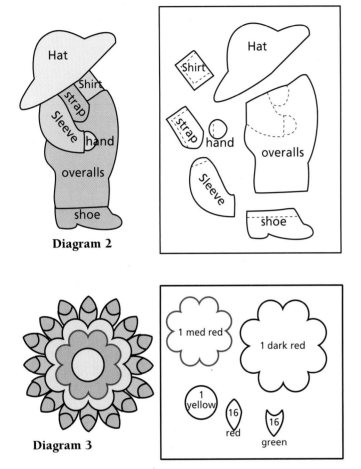

Diagram 2

Diagram 3

Trace pattern pieces that will be cut from the same fabric at the same time. (**Diagram 4**) It will make cutting easier and will be a more efficient use of fusible product and fabric.

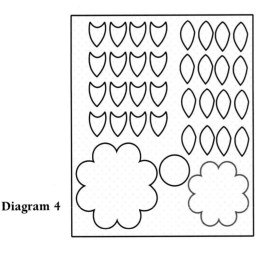

Diagram 4

Cut out the pattern sections from the fusible web, and fuse to wrong side of appropriate fabric following manufacturer's directions. (**Diagram 5**)

Diagram 5

Cut out appliqué pieces along drawn line. (**Diagram 6**)

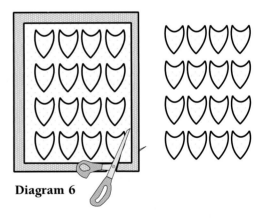

Diagram 6

Hint: If you are going to cut out all appliqué pieces for your quilt at one time, place pieces for each block in its own recloseable plastic bag.

MAKING APPLIQUÉ BLOCKS

For any of the quilts in this book, cut background squares 9½" x 9½".

Fold square in half, then in half again; finger press along folds. (**Diagram 7**)

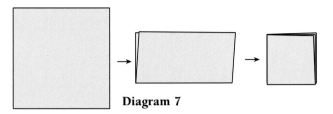

Diagram 7

Place background square on ironing surface. Position appliqué pieces on background square referring to block photo. Use center lines on patterns and folds in background square as guides for placement. (**Diagram 8**)

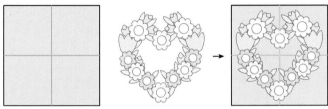

Diagram 8

Hint: If you are not comfortable placing your appliqué pieces, trace full-size pattern onto a piece of clear template plastic or mylar using a dark permanent marker. Place background square right side up on ironing surface with traced pattern centered on fabric. (**Diagram 9**) Position appliqué pieces on background under the template guide; lift the clear pattern guide carefully as you go. Readjust pieces until desired placement is achieved.

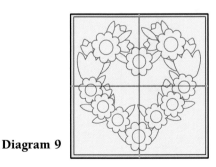

Diagram 9

Important: *Since some of the blocks are not symmetrical, they will end up as mirror images to the actual pattern. You will need to flop the traced pattern before positioning appliqué pieces.*

When you are satisfied with the placement of your appliqué pieces, fuse to background following manufacturer's directions.

OPTIONAL MACHINE APPLIQUÉ

If you would like to machine stitch around edges of appliqué pieces, use a machine zigzag or blanket stitch. Use invisible nylon monofilament thread so you will not have to continually change thread color. (**Diagram 10**)

Diagram 10

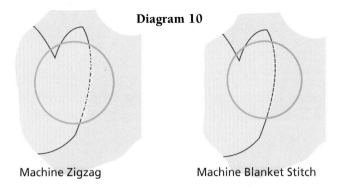

Machine Zigzag   Machine Blanket Stitch

SEWING BLOCKS TOGETHER

Place blocks referring to photographed quilts and layouts.

Sew blocks together in rows and then sew rows together. Press lightly and carefully. Too much pressing may cause some fusible products to melt.

ADDING BORDERS

Simple Borders
Measure quilt top lengthwise. Cut border strips to that length.

If quilt top is longer than the width of your fabric, you will need to piece the strips. To make the joining seam less noticeable, sew strips together diagonally. Place two strips right sides together at right angles. Sew a diagonal seam. (**Diagram 11**)

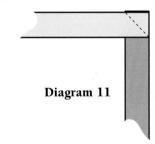

Diagram 11

Trim excess fabric ¼" from stitching. (**Diagram 12**)

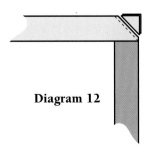

Diagram 12

Press seam open. (**Diagram 13**)

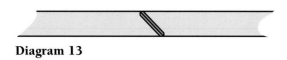

Diagram 13

Cut border strips the measured length.

Sew border strips to sides of quilt top. Press seams toward border strips.

Measure quilt top crosswise including borders just added. Cut border strips that length and sew to top and bottom of quilt top.

Repeat for any other borders.

Mitered Borders

Mitered borders are more time-consuming than the simple borders described above and you may not finish your quilt top in 48 hours. But when using a floral strip print as in the Faux Baltimore Album, page 20, it is well worth the effort.

Measure the quilt top lengthwise. Cut (and piece if necessary) two strips that length plus twice the finished border width plus 1/2" for seam allowances. (Example: For a quilt 64" x 64" with an 8"-wide finished border, you will need to cut the border strips, 64 + 8 + 8 + 1/2" or 801/2".)

Measure the quilt top crosswise. Cut (and piece if necessary) two strips that length plus twice the finished border width plus 1/2".

Find the midpoint of a border strip by folding strip in half. (**Diagram 14**)

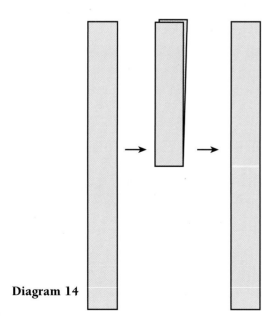

Diagram 14

Place strip right side together with quilt top matching midpoint of border with midpoint of quilt side. (**Diagram 15**) Pin in place.

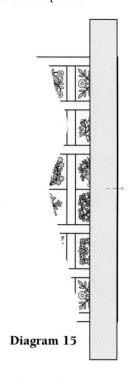

Diagram 15

Pin border to quilt top along entire side.

Beginning 1/4" from top edge, sew border strip to quilt top ending 1/4" from bottom edge. Backstitch at beginning and ending of sewing. (**Diagram 16**)

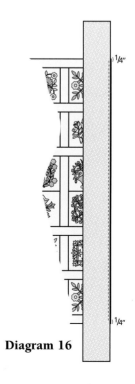

1/4"

1/4"

Diagram 16

Repeat at remaining three sides.

To finish corners, fold quilt top in half diagonally; borders will extend straight up and away from quilt.

Place a ruler along folded edge of quilt top, going into border strip; draw a diagonal line on border. (**Diagram 17**)

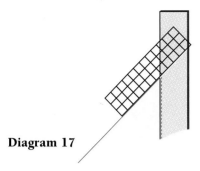

Diagram 17

Beginning at corner of quilt top, stitch along drawn line to edge of border strip. (**Diagram 18**)

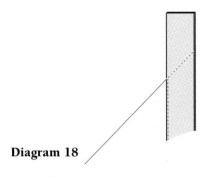

Diagram 18

Open quilt at corner to check miter. If satisfied, trim excess fabric ¼" from diagonal seam. (**Diagram 19**)

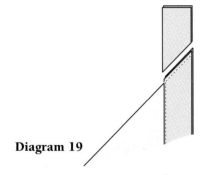

Diagram 19

Repeat process at remaining three corners.

FINISHING YOUR QUILT

Attaching the Batting and Backing

There are a number of different types of batting on the market today including the new fusible battings that eliminate the need for basting. Your choice of batting will depend upon how you are planning to use your quilt. If the quilt is to serve as a wall hanging, you will probably want to use a thin cotton batting. A quilt made with a thin cotton or cotton/polyester blend works best for machine quilting. Very thick polyester batting should be used only for tied quilts.

The best fabric for quilt backing is 100% cotton fabric. If your quilt is larger than the available fabric you will have to piece your backing fabric. When joining the fabric, try not to have a seam going down the center. Instead cut off the selvages and make a center strip that is about 36" wide and have narrower strips at the sides. Seam the pieces together and carefully iron the seams open. (This is one of the few times in making a quilt that a seam should be pressed open.) Several fabric manufacturers are now selling fabric in 90" or 108"-widths for use as backing fabric.

It is a good idea to remove the batting from its wrapping 24 hours before you plan to use it and open it out to full size. You will find that the batting will now lie flat when you are ready to use it.

The batting and the backing should be cut about one to two inches larger on all sides than the quilt top. Place the backing wrong side up on a flat surface. Smooth out the batting on top of this, matching the outer edges. Center the quilt top, right side up, on top of the batting.

Now the quilt layers must be held together before quilting, and there are several methods for doing this:

Safety-pin Basting: Starting from the center and working toward the edges, pin through all layers at one time with large safety pins. The pins should be placed no more than 4" apart. As you work, think of your quilting plan to make sure that the pins will avoid prospective quilting lines.

Thread Basting: Baste the three layers together with long stitches. Start in the center and sew toward the edges in a number of diagonal lines.

Quilt-gun Basting: This handy trigger tool pushes nylon tags through all layers of the quilt. Start in the center and work toward the outside edges. The tags should be placed about 4" apart. You can sew right over the tags, which can then be easily removed by cutting them off with scissors.

Spray or Heat-set Basting: Several manufacturers have spray adhesives available especially for quilters. Apply these products by following the manufacturer's directions. You might want to test these products before you use them to make sure that they meet your requirements.

Fusible Iron-on Basting: These battings are a wonderful new way to hold quilt layers together without using any of the other time-consuming methods of basting. Again, you will want to test these battings to be certain that you are happy with the results. Follow the manufacturer's directions.

Quilting

If you like the process of hand quilting, you can—of course—finish these projects by hand quilting. However, if you want to finish these quilts quickly, in the time we are suggesting, you will want to use a sewing machine for quilting.

If you have never used a sewing machine for quilting, you may want to find a book and read about the technique. You do not need a special machine for quilting. Just make sure that your machine has been oiled and is in good working condition.

If you are going to do machine quilting, you should invest in an even-feed foot. This foot is designed to feed the top and bottom layers of a quilt evenly through the machine. The foot prevents puckers from forming as you machine quilt. Use a fine transparent nylon thread in the top and regular sewing thread in the bobbin.

Quilting in the ditch is one of the easiest ways to machine quilt. This is a term used to describe stitching along the seam line between two pieces of fabric. Using your fingers, pull the blocks or pieces apart slightly and machine stitch right between the two pieces. The stitching will look better if you keep the stitching to the side of the seam that does not have the extra bulk of the seam allowance under it. The quilting will be hidden in the seam.

Free-form machine quilting can be used to quilt around a design or to quilt a motif. The quilting is done with a darning foot and the feed dogs down on the sewing machine. It takes practice to master free-form quilting because you are controlling the movement of the quilt under the needle rather than the sewing machine moving the quilt. You can quilt in any direction—up and down, side-to-side and even in circles—without pivoting the quilt around the needle. Practice this quilting method before trying it on your quilt.

Attaching the Continuous Machine Binding

Once the quilt has been quilted, the edges must be bound. Start by trimming the backing and batting even with the quilt top. Measure the quilt top and cut enough 2¹⁄₂" wide strips to go around all four sides of the quilt plus 12". Join the strips end to end with diagonal seams

and trim the corners. Press the seams open. (**Diagram 20**)

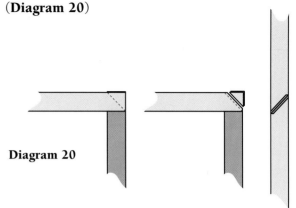

Diagram 20

Cut one end of the strip at a 45-degree angle and press under ¹⁄₄". Press entire strip in half lengthwise, wrong sides together. (**Diagram 21**)

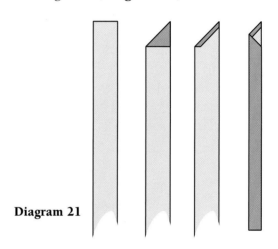

Diagram 21

On the back of the quilt, position the binding in the middle of one side, keeping the raw edges together. Sew the binding to the quilt with a ¹⁄₄" seam allowance, beginning about 3" below the folded end of the binding. (**Diagram 22**)

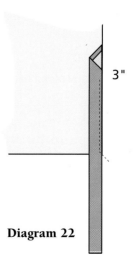

3"

Diagram 22

At the corner, stop ¼" from the edge of the quilt and backstitch; cut threads.

Fold binding away from quilt so it is at a right angle to edge just sewn. (**Diagram 23**)

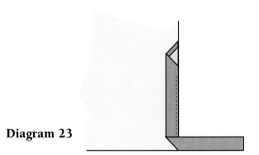

Diagram 23

Then, fold the binding back on itself so the fold is on the quilt edge and the raw edges are aligned with the adjacent side of the quilt. Begin sewing at the quilt edge. (**Diagram 24**)

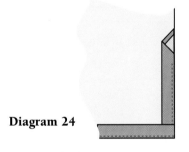

Diagram 24

Continue in the same way around the remaining sides of the quilt. Stop about 2" away from the starting point. Trim any excess binding and tuck it inside the folded end. Finish the stitching. (**Diagram 25**)

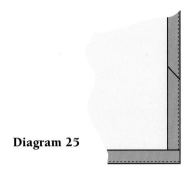

Diagram 25

Fold and press the binding to the front of the quilt so the seam line is covered; machine-stitch the binding in place on the front of the quilt. Use a straight stitch or tiny zigzag with invisible or matching thread. If you have a sewing machine that does embroidery stitches, you may want to use your favorite stitch.

Always sign and date your quilt when finished. You can make a label by cross-stitching or embroidering or even writing on a label or on the back of your quilt with a permanent marking pen. If you are friends with your computer, you can even create an attractive label on the computer.

EASY APPLIQUÉ

A great beginner's project that alternates simple-to-make appliqué blocks with your favorite floral or novelty print.

Approximate Size: 58" x 76"

Patterns (pages 23 to 39)**:** Blocks 1 to 17

MATERIALS

½ yard blue (appliqués)

½ yard dark turquoise (appliqués)

1½ yards white (background)

1½ yards coordinating print (alternate blocks)

½ yard green (first border)

1¼ yards coordinating print (second border)

⅝ yard print (binding)

4 yards backing

Twin-size batting

1½ yards paper-backed fusible product

CUTTING

Blocks

17 squares, 9½" x 9½", white (background)

18 squares, 9½" x 9½", coordinating print
  (alternate blocks)

Finishing

6 strips, green, 2"-wide x width (first border)

7 strips, print, 5½"-wide x width (second
  border)

7 strips, print, 2½"-wide x width (binding)

INSTRUCTIONS

1. Refer to Preparing Appliqué Pieces, pages 3 and 4, to cut out pieces for blocks 1 to 17.

2. Following manufacturer's directions and referring to Making Appliqué Blocks, page 5, fuse block pieces to background squares. Machine stitch around appliqué pieces if desired.

3. Referring to Layout, place appliqué blocks alternating with print squares in seven rows of five.

4. Sew blocks together in rows, then sew rows together.

5. For first border, measure quilt lengthwise. Cut two 2"-wide green border strips to that length and sew to sides of quilt. Measure quilt crosswise. Cut two 2"-wide green border strips to that length and sew to top and bottom of quilt.

6. For second border, repeat step 5 with 5½"-wide coordinating print strips.

7. Layer, quilt and add binding referring to Finishing Your Quilt, pages 7 to 9.

Easy Appliqué Quilt Layout

FAVORITE THINGS

Delight a child with appliquéd flannel motifs; the perfect gift for the brand new baby.

Approximate Size: 51" x 51"
Patterns (pages 40 to 49): Blocks 18 to 27

MATERIALS

½ yard pink (background and pieced triangles)

⅝ yard yellow (background, pieced triangles and corner triangles)

⅝ yard blue (background)

Assorted flannel fat quarters, white, medium gray, dark gray, light brown, light blue, medium blue, light pink, medium pink, green, and yellow (appliqués)

½ yard blue (first border)

⅞ yard yellow (second border)

½ yard yellow (binding)

2½ yards backing

Twin-size batting

1 yard paper-backed fusible web

permanent fabric markers or embroidery floss

CUTTING

Blocks

1 square, 9½" x 9½", yellow

8 squares, 9½" x 9½", blue

4 squares, 9½" x 9½", pink

8 squares, 4½" x 4½", pink

Finishing

4 squares, 8½" x 8½", yellow, cut in quarters diagonally (pieced triangles)

2 squares, 8" x 8", yellow, cut in half diagonally (corner triangles)

5 strips, 2½" x width, blue (first border)

6 strips, 4½" x width, yellow (second border)

6 strips, 2½" x width, yellow (binding)

INSTRUCTIONS

1. Refer to Preparing the Appliqué Pieces, pages 3 and 4, to cut out pieces for blocks 19 to 27 and pieces for four block 18 from fabric and paper-backed fusible web.

2. Following manufacturer's directions and referring to Making Appliqué Blocks, page 5, fuse block pieces to background squares diagonally as follows: block 19 on yellow square, block 18 on pink squares, and remaining blocks (20 to 27) on blue squares. Add block design details using permanent fabric markers or embroidery floss.

3. For pieced finishing triangles, sew a small yellow triangle to a 4½" pink square. (**Diagram 1**) Note that the triangle is larger than the square. Sew another small triangle to adjacent side of square to complete pieced finishing triangle. (**Diagram 2**) Note that the triangles are oversized.

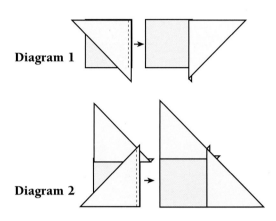

Diagram 1

Diagram 2

4. Repeat step 3 for seven more pieced finishing triangles.

5. Place blocks and pieced finishing triangles in diagonal rows. (**Diagram 3**) Sew blocks together.

Diagram 3

6. Sew rows together. Sew large yellow triangles to corners last. (**Diagram 4**)

7. Square up quilt top by trimming sides ¼" out from points of Heart blocks. (**Diagram 5**)

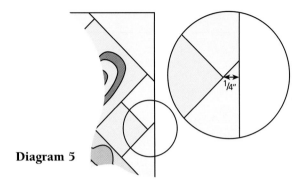

Diagram 5

8. For first border, measure quilt lengthwise. Cut two 2½"-wide blue strips to that length and sew to sides of quilt. Measure quilt crosswise. Cut two 2½"-wide blue strips to that length and sew to top and bottom of quilt.

9. For second border, repeat step 8 for 4½"-wide yellow strips.

10. Layer, quilt and add binding referring to Finishing Your Quilt, pages 7 to 9.

Diagram 4

Favorite Things Quilt Layout

HEARTS AND FLOWERS

A subtle heart background showcases eight different heart blocks, each done in two color ways.

Approximate Size: 45" x 45"
Patterns (pages 50 to 57): Blocks 28 to 35

MATERIALS

5/8 yard light pink (background)

1 yard medium pink (background)

Assorted fat quarters, light, medium, and dark pink (appliqués)

Assorted fat quarters, light and dark green, gold (appliqués)

3/8 yard green (first border)

5/8 yard medium pink (second border)

1/2 yard medium pink (binding)

1½ yard backing

Crib-size batting

1½ yards paper-backed fusible web

CUTTING

Blocks

2 squares, 9½" x 9½", light pink

8 squares, 9½" x 9½", medium pink

3 squares, 9⅞" x 9⅞", light pink (cut in half diagonally)

3 squares, 9⅞" x 9⅞", medium pink (cut in half diagonally)

Finishing

4 strips, 2" x width, green (first border)

5 strips, 3½" x width, medium pink (second border)

5 strips, 2½" x width, medium pink (binding)

INSTRUCTIONS

1. Sew a light and a medium pink triangle together to form background square. (**Diagram 1**) Press seam open. Trim block to 9½" square. Make six light/medium background squares.

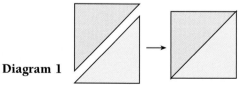

Diagram 1

2. Refer to Preparing Appliqué Pieces, pages 3 and 4, to cut out pieces for two of each block 28 to 35.

3. Following manufacturer's directions and referring to Making Appliqué Blocks, page 5, fuse block pieces to background squares. Fuse Blocks 30 and 33 to light pink background and blocks 28 to 35 to medium pink background. Fuse blocks 28, 29, 31, 32, 34, and 35 to light/medium pink triangle square backgrounds, noting position of triangles. Machine stitch around appliqué pieces if desired.

4. Place blocks in four rows of four blocks. (**Diagram 2**)

Diagram 2

Note that the correct placement of blocks form a heart background. (**Diagram 3**)

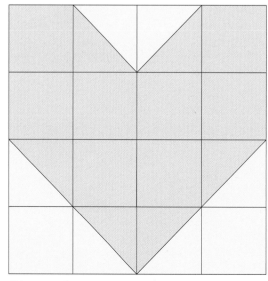

Diagram 3

5. Sew blocks together in rows, then sew rows together.

6. For first border, measure quilt lengthwise. Cut two 2"-wide green border strips to that length and sew to sides of quilt. Measure quilt crosswise. Cut two 2"-wide green border strips to that length and sew to top and bottom of quilt.

7. For second border, repeat step 6 with 3½"-wide medium pink strips.

8. Layer, quilt and add binding referring to Finishing Your Quilt, pages 7 to 9.

Hearts and Flowers Quilt Layout

17

CHRISTMAS ROSES

Make these luscious rose blocks in Christmas red and green for a spectacular addition to your holiday décor, or choose other colors for a year-around charming quilt.

Approximate Size: 54" x 54"

Patterns (pages 58 to 70)**:** Blocks 36 to 48

MATERIALS

1/4 yard each of three red prints (appliqués)

1/4 yard each of three green prints (appliqués)

Fat quarter blue print (appliqués)

Fat quarter each of two gold prints (appliqués)

1 1/2 yards dark gold (background)

1 1/4 yards light gold (background)

1/2 yard red (first border)

3/4 yard Christmas print (second border)

5/8 yard red (binding)

3 1/2 yards backing

Twin-size batting

2 yards paper-backed fusible product

CUTTING

Blocks

13 squares, 9 1/2" x 9 1/2", dark gold

12 squares, 9 1/2" x 9 1/2", light gold

Finishing

5 strips, 2"-wide x width, red (first border)

6 strips, 3 1/2"-wide x width, Christmas print (second border)

6 strips, 2 1/2"-wide x width, red (binding)

INSTRUCTIONS

1. Refer to Preparing Appliqué Pieces, pages 3 and 4, to cut out pieces for blocks 36 to 48. Note that there are four of blocks 38, 43, 47 and 48.

2. Following manufacturer's directions and referring to Making Appliqué Blocks, page 5, fuse block pieces for blocks to 38, 41, 43, and 47 on dark gold squares and blocks 36, 37, 39, 40, 42, 44, 45, 46, and 48 on light gold squares. Machine stitch around appliqué pieces if desired.

3. Place blocks in five rows of five blocks noting placement of light and dark gold background squares. (**Diagram 1**)

4. Sew blocks together in rows, then sew rows together.

5. For first border, measure quilt lengthwise. Cut two 2"-wide red border strips to that length and sew to sides of quilt. Measure quilt crosswise. Cut two 2"-wide red border strips to that length and sew to top and bottom of quilt.

Diagram 1

6. For second border, repeat step 5 with 3 1/2"-wide Christmas print strips.

7. Layer, quilt and add binding referring to Finishing Your Quilt, pages 7 to 9.

Christmas Roses Quilt Layout

18

FAUX BALTIMORE ALBUM

Always wanted to make a Baltimore Album Quilt but were afraid to try?
Try a faux quilt with fused squares using fabrics from Marti Michell's Rose Garden by Maywood Studio.

Approximate Size: 82" x 82"
Patterns (pages 71 to 96): Blocks 49 to 74

MATERIALS

2½ yards off-white tone-on-tone print (background)
Assorted fat quarters, shades of pink, purple, blue, peach, green, gold (appliqués)
*1½ yards off-white print (sashing)
2½ yards floral print (border)
⅝ yard off-white tone-on-tone print (binding)
6 yards backing
Queen-size batting
3½ yards paper-backed fusible web

CUTTING

Blocks
36 squares, 9½" x 9½", off-white tone-on-tone print

Finishing
16 strips, 2½" x 9½", off-white print (sashing)
4 strips, 2½" x 18½", off-white print (sashing)
*6 strips, 2½" x 62½", off-white print (sashing)
*2 strips, 2½" x 66½", off-white print (sashing)
9 strips, 8½" x width (or 4 strips, 8½" x length), floral (border)
9 strips, 2½" x width, off-white tone-on-tone print (binding)
*Fabric strips must be pieced and cut to achieve desired length. Refer to page 5 for piecing strips diagonally.

INSTRUCTIONS

1. Refer to Preparing Appliqué Pieces, pages 3 and 4, to cut out pieces for four Block 68, eight Block 70 and one each of remaining blocks.

2. Following manufacturer's directions and referring to Making Appliqué Blocks, page 5, fuse block pieces to background squares. Machine stitch around appliqué pieces if desired.

3. Place blocks in six rows of six blocks. Fit sashing strips in between. Note that there is no sashing between the third and fourth blocks.

4. Sew blocks and 2½" x 9½" sashing strips together for rows 1, 2, 5 and 6. (**Diagram 1**)

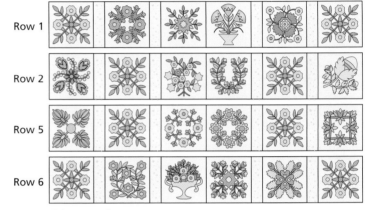

Diagram 1

5. For rows 3 and 4, sew the blocks together in pairs vertically. (**Diagram 2**)

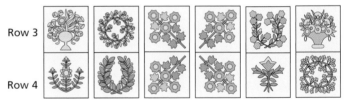

Diagram 2

6. Sew the row 3/4 pairs together with 2½" x 18½" sashing strips in between. (**Diagram 3**) Note that there is no sashing between the third and fourth pair of blocks.

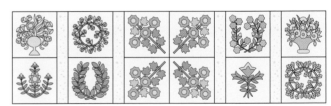

Diagram 3

7. Sew rows together with 2½" x 62½" sashing strips in between. (**Diagram 4**)

8. Sew 2½" x 62½" sashing strips to sides of quilt. Sew 2½" x 66½" sashing strips to top and bottom. (**Diagram 5**)

Diagram 4

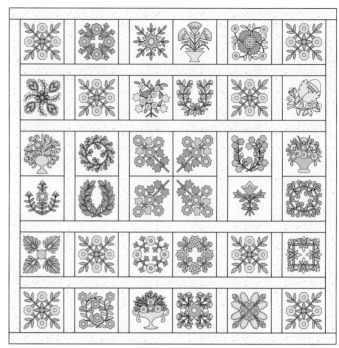

Diagram 5

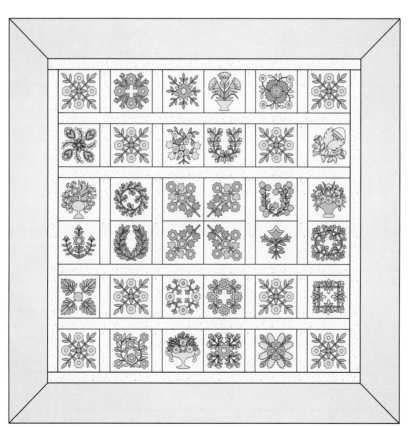

Faux Baltimore Album Quilt Layout

9. The photographed quilt has a mitered border using a floral stripe print. Measure the quilt top crosswise and lengthwise. Cut four strips that length plus the width of two borders plus ½" seam allowance. For example, the quilt should measure 66" x 66", and the finidhed border strips are 8" wide, so cut the strips 66" + 8" + 8" + ½" = 82½".

10. Refer to Mitered Borders, pages 6 to 7, to add border.

11. Layer, quilt and add binding referring to Finishing Your Quilt, pages 7 to 9.

2 EASY APPLIQUÉ
Four-leaf Clover

25

5 EASY APPLIQUÉ
Starflower

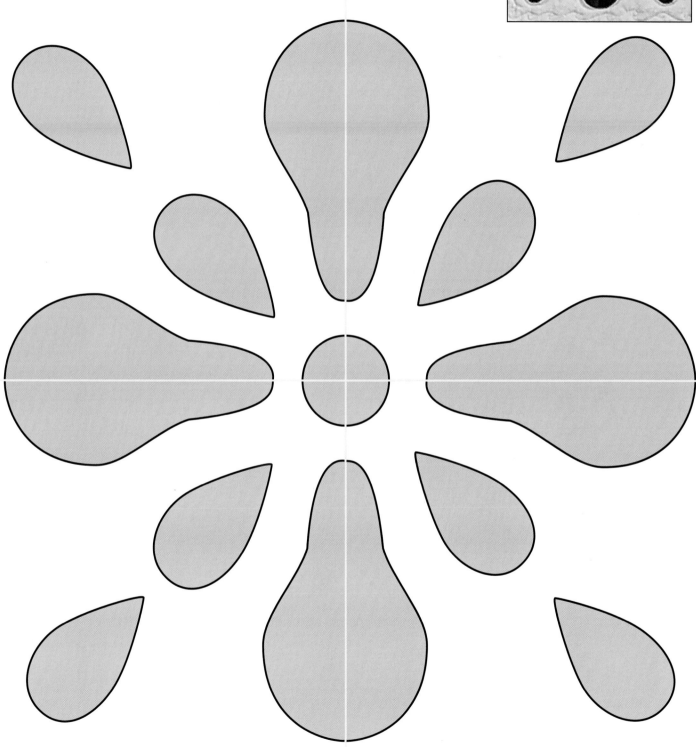

29

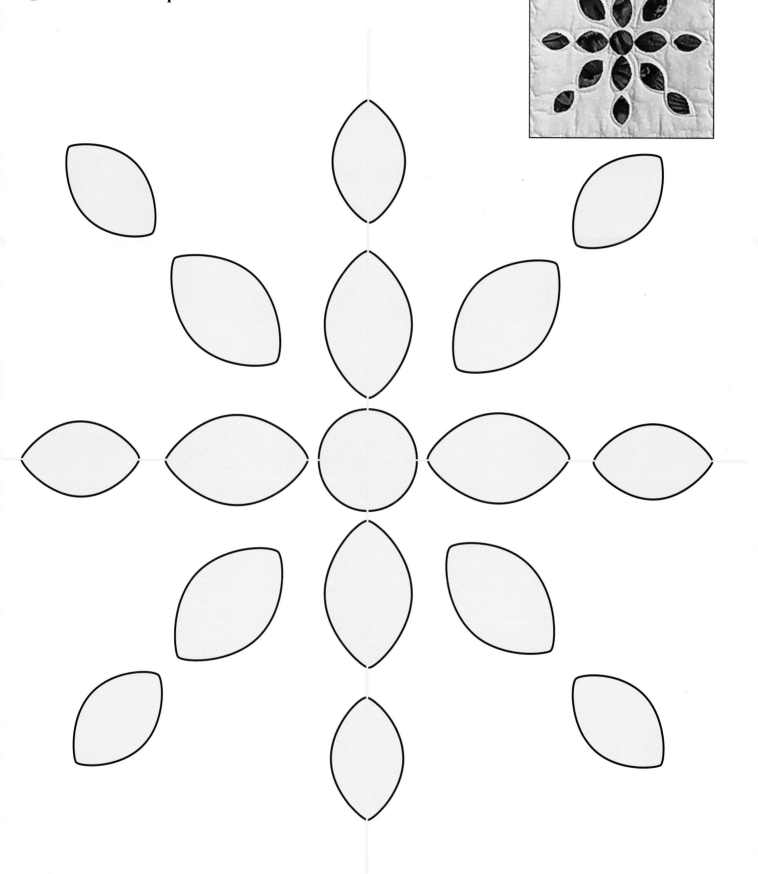

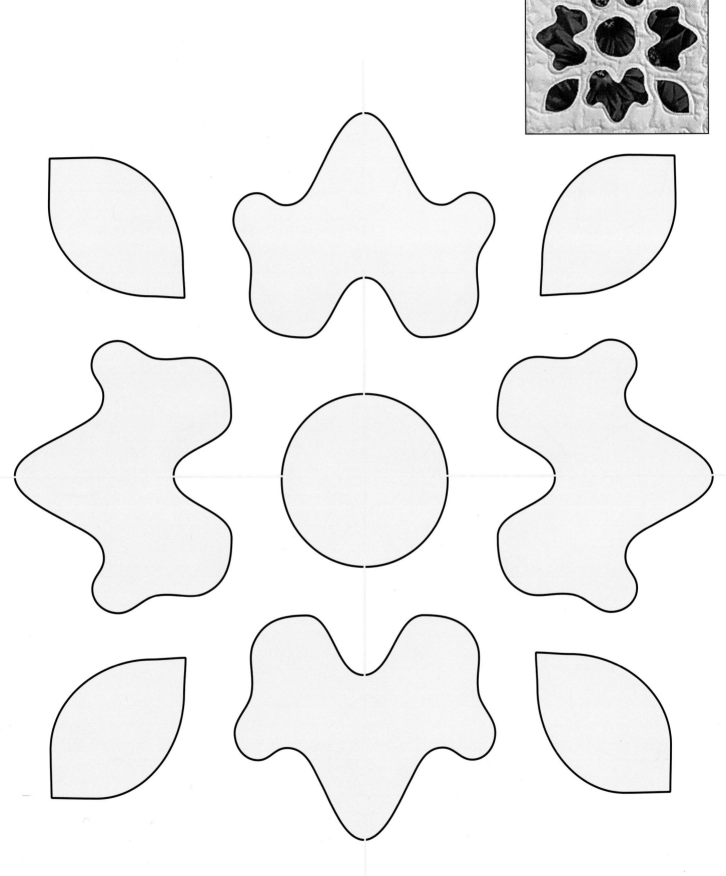

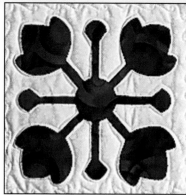

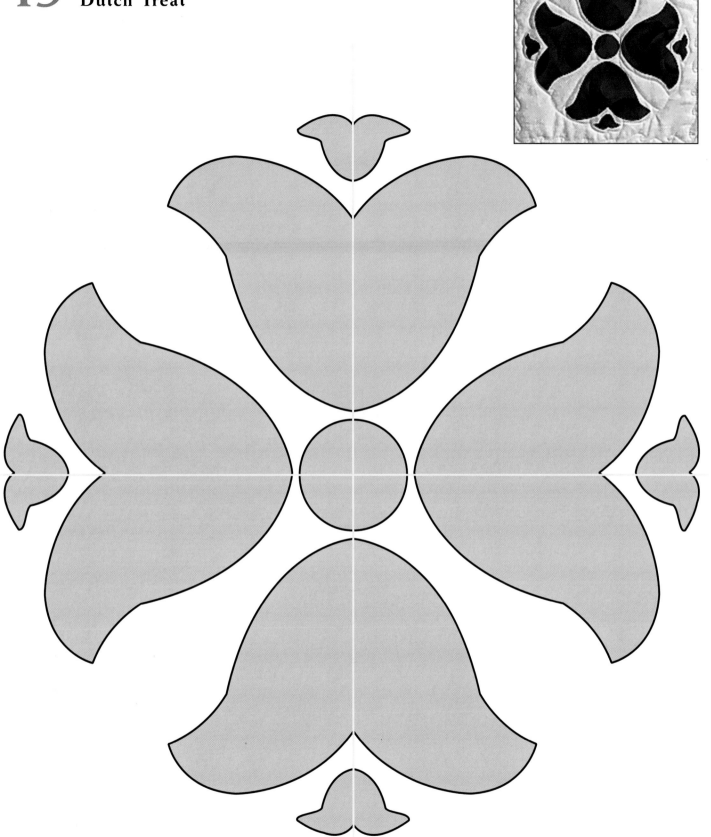

16 EASY APPLIQUÉ
Ink Blot

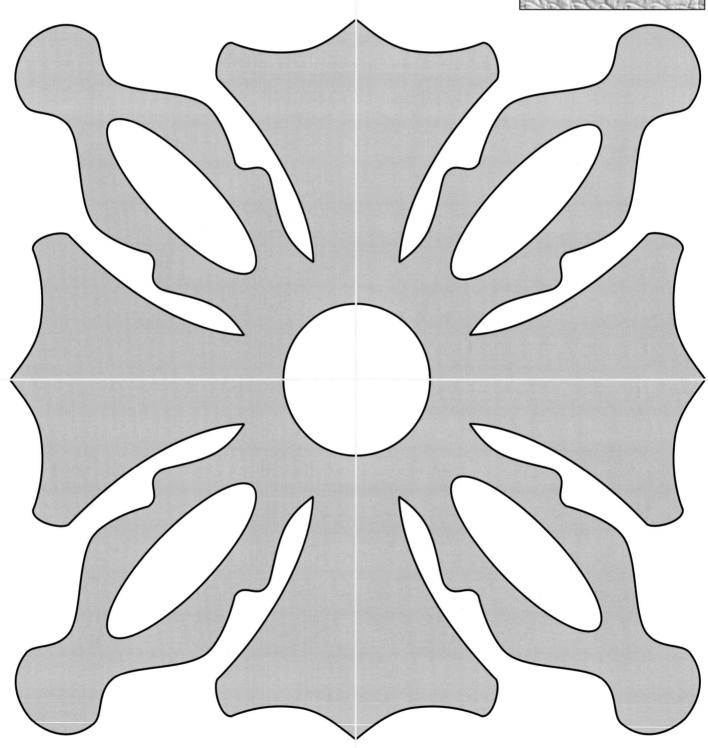

17 EASY APPLIQUÉ
Framed Snowflake

40

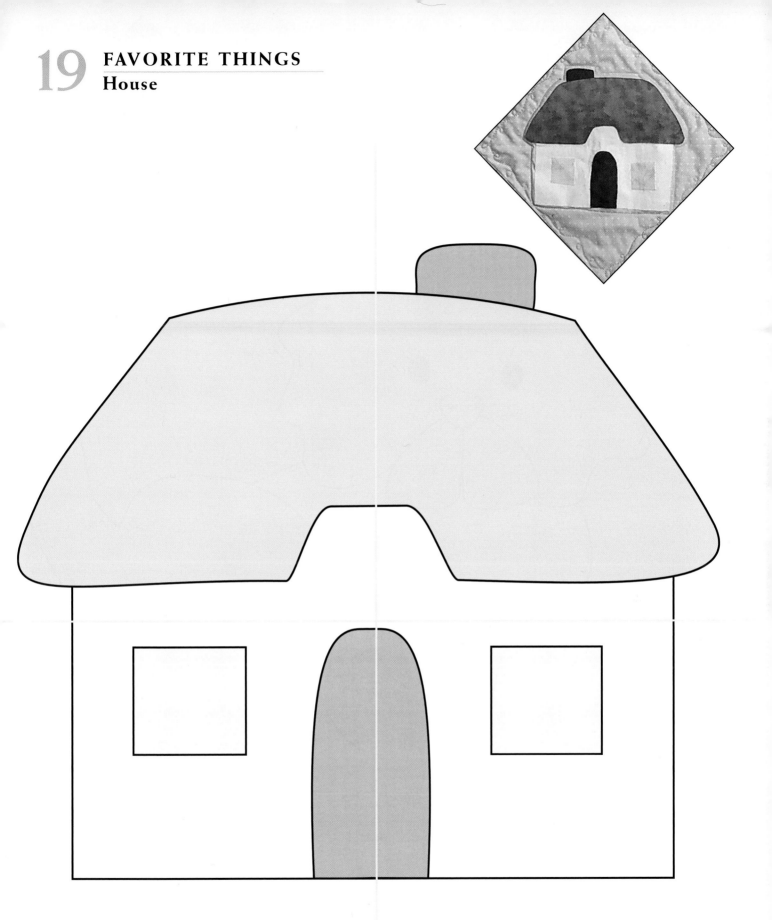

22 FAVORITE THINGS
Overall Sam

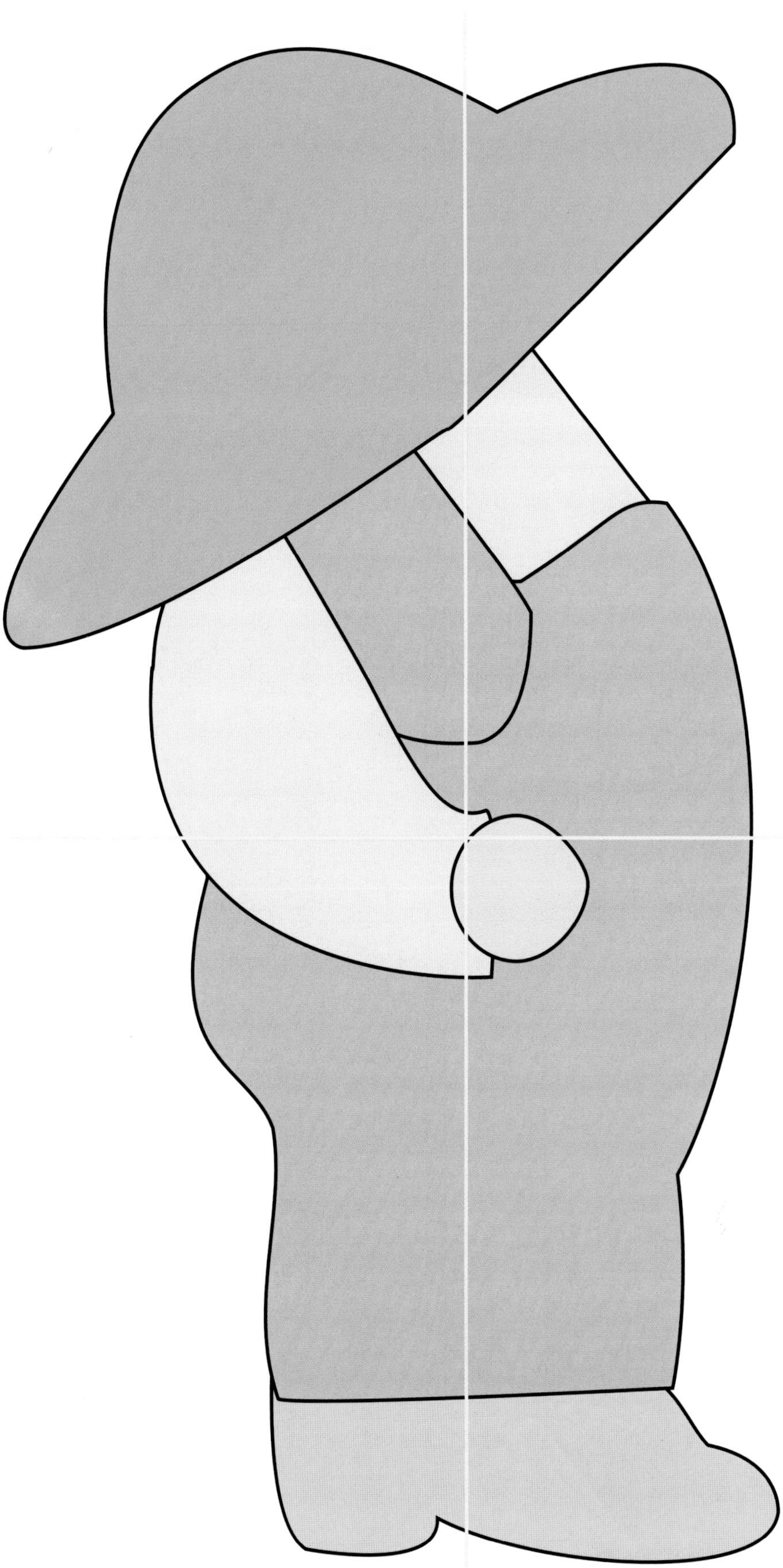

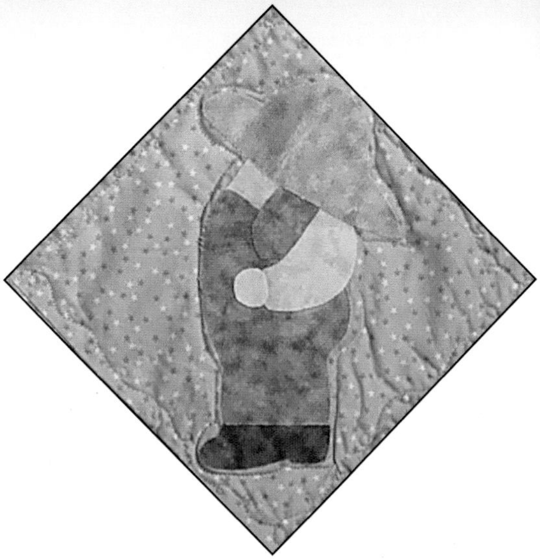

30 HEARTS AND FLOWERS
Love Birds

Hint: Since many pattern pieces are similar in size and shape, label pattern pieces to make placement easier.

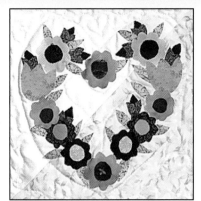

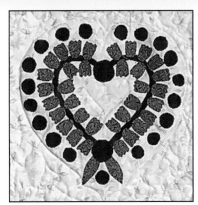

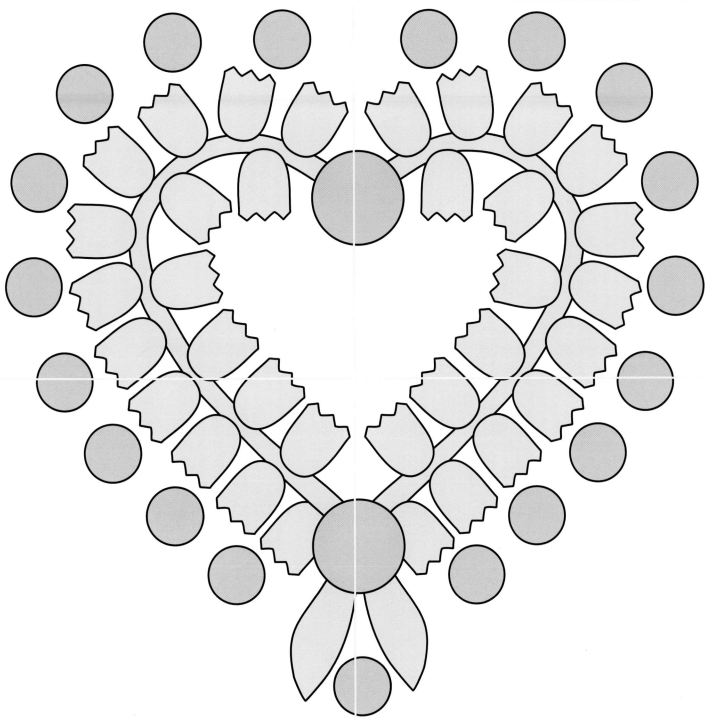

HEARTS AND FLOWERS
Sweetheart

Hint: Since many pattern pieces are similar in size and shape, label pattern pieces to make placement easier.

36 CHRISTMAS ROSES
Mrs. Potter's Rose

38 CHRISTMAS ROSES
Rose Bouquet

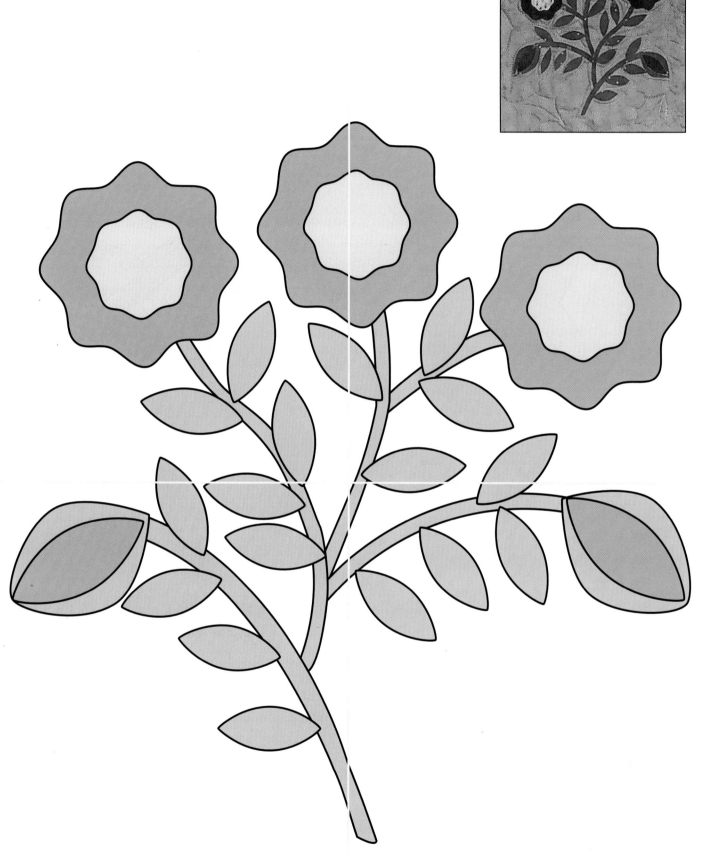

41 CHRISTMAS ROSES
Sadie's Choice

CHRISTMAS ROSES
Whig Rose

43 CHRISTMAS ROSES
Album Roses

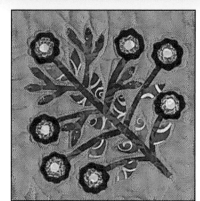

CHRISTMAS ROSES
Wreath of Roses

CHRISTMAS ROSES
Mrs. Kretsinger's Rose

48 CHRISTMAS ROSES
Harrison Rose

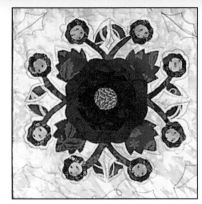

FAUX BALTIMORE ALBUM
Floral Bowl

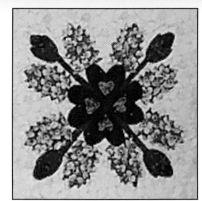

FAUX BALTIMORE ALBUM
Grape Vine

FAUX BALTIMORE ALBUM
Budding Vine

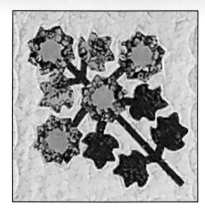

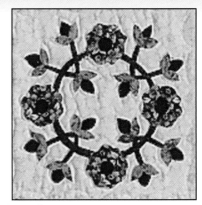

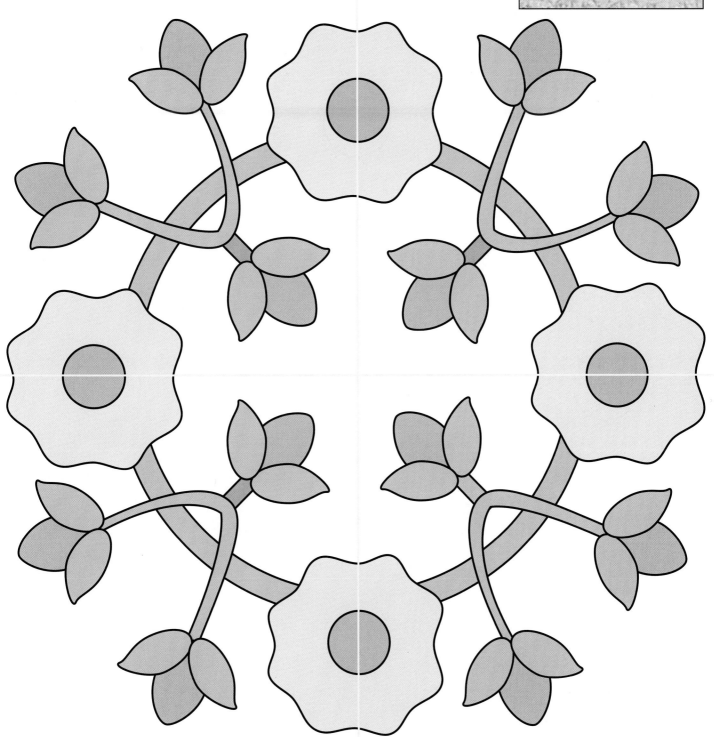

93

FAUX BALTIMORE ALBUM
Purple Posies